ᚱᚢᚾᛖᛗᚨᚷᛁᚲ ᛏᚢᛟᚢᚱᛋᚤ

Suppressed and n Church, runes ar among serious ma the magical purpo possess unique qu invoking the powe ing them into cere you direct control over the actions of the Norse deities!

Each runic symbol contains an elemental force which corresponds to a god or natural power. Whether using runes for ritual magic, meditation or divination, the forces set in motion by runes are primal and highly effective. However, before they can be effective for works of magic or divination, they must be understood on the intuitive level. This book explains how to form runes on the astral level to bring to life in your unconscious.

Find out which runes are most appropriate for you— tap the primal energy of the wild Northern gods — empower a rune amulet to help you achieve material goals or use rune wands, stones, cards or dice to divine your future. All of them are clearly explained in this resourceful book!

Runes are the ultimate magical tool for ritual work with the Northern deities. The recent rediscovery of the runes is the single most important event in occultism in the twentieth century. *The Truth About Runes* will show you just why!

About the Author

Donald Tyson is a Canadian from Halifax, Nova Scotia. He devotes his life to the attainment of a complete gnosis of the art of magic in theory and practice. His purpose is to formulate an accessible system of personal training composed of East and West, past and present, that will help individuals discover the reasons for their existence and ways to fulfill it.

To Write to the Author

If you wish to contact the author or would like more information about this book, please write to the author in care of Llewellyn Worldwide and we will forward your request. Both the author and publisher appreciate hearing from you and learning of your enjoyment of this book and how it has helped you. Llewellyn Worldwide cannot guarantee that every letter written to the author will be answered, but all will be forwarded. Please write to:

Donald Tyson
c/o Llewellyn Worldwide
P.O. Box 64383-829, St. Paul, MN 55164-0383, U.S.A.

Please enclose a self-addressed, stamped envelope for reply, or $1.00 to cover costs.
If outside U.S.A., enclose International Postal Reply coupon.

Free Catalog From Llewellyn

For more than ninety years Llewellyn has brought its readers knowledge in the fields of metaphysics and human potential. Learn about the newest books in spiritual guidance, natural healing, astrology, occult philosophy and more. Enjoy book reviews, New Age articles, a calendar of events, plus current products and services. To get your free copy of *Llewellyn's New Worlds of Mind and Spirit*, send your name and address to:

Llewellyn's New Worlds of Mind and Spirit
P.O. Box 64383-829, St. Paul, MN 55164-0383, U.S.A.

LLEWELLYN'S VANGUARD SERIES

The Truth About

Runes

by Donald Tyson

1995
Llewellyn Publications
St. Paul, MN 55164-0383, U.S.A.

For permissions, serialization, condensation, or adaptations, write to the publisher.

FIRST EDITION, 1989
SECOND EDITION
First Printing, 1995

Cover photograph by Michael Dvorak

International Standard Book Number:
0-87542-829-0

LLEWELLYN PUBLICATIONS
A Division of Llewellyn Worldwide, Ltd.
P.O. Box 64383, St. Paul, MN 55164-0383, U.S.A.

Other Books by Donald Tyson

The New Magus, 1988
Rune Magic, 1988
The Truth About Ritual Magic, 1989
How to Make and Use a Magic Mirror, 1990
Ritual Magic, 1991
The Messenger, 1993

Cards and Kits by Donald Tyson

Rune Magic Deck, 1988
Power of the Runes, 1989

Editor and Annotator

*Three Books of Occult Philosophy written by Henry
    Cornelius Agrippa Von Nettesheim, 1993*

Forthcoming:

Tetragrammaton

THE TRUTH ABOUT RUNES

WHAT ARE RUNES?

From a word to a word I was led to a word,
From a deed to another deed.

—Havamal

The runes are a set of symbols that concisely
embody the most potent magical system of the
ancient world. Because rune magic was rarely
described in written records, persecution by the
Catholic Church during the Middle Ages succeeded
in obliterating almost the entire tradition of rune
use from the memories of the peoples of northern
Europe, the indigenous home of the runes. Runes
became the recreation of antiquarian scholars,
known only as an obscure and obsolete alphabet
preserved in crumbling parchment manuscripts
and on leaning stone monuments erected by the
vanished Vikings.

Runic characters are letters that can be used for
writing. This is their exoteric function. But in pagan
times they were used for much more. The undi-
vided forest wilderness in which the wandering
Germanic tribes hunted and made war upon each
other was ruled by elemental forces—water, sun,
storm, the seasons, trees, the bull, the horse, fire on
the hearthstones, the cleared camp circle, the human
virtues of cunning speech, courage and battle skill,

the mysteries of birth, growth and death—all of which combined together to determine the lives of frail human beings.

The German god *Donar*, called by the Norsemen *Thor*, can be traced back to the Sun. *Woden*, or *Odin*, was originally the fury of the storm. *Ing*, the deity who gives England its name, sprang from the fertility of the Earth. All the major Teutonic gods are based upon a limited number of natural potencies. Although they were later refined and made more human in poetry and art, in earliest days they were different masks of the ever-changing face of nature.

The Germanic tribes embodied these same elemental forces in simple symbols that were used for works of magic and divination by the shamans, who served the combined functions of magician-physician-priest. By making symbols to represent the most important powers of the world, these powers could be manipulated for conscious human purposes. The symbols formed the magical link between men and the blind gods of nature, and allowed the shamans to control the destinies of their tribes.

Runes are descendants of these shamanic power symbols, whose origins extend deep into the past, before the beginnings of writing. Each rune is both a letter and a vessel of natural potency. There is a rune for water and a rune for earth, a rune for hail and a rune for ice, a rune for horse and a rune for man. There are also runes that name some of the Teutonic gods. Ing has his own rune, as does *Woden* (Os) and *Tiw* (*Tyr*). These runes represent both the gods and the natural potencies upon which the gods are based. For example, the rune for Tiw is both the god Tiw and the human virtues of honor and courage.

It may be that at one time all runes were the symbols of recognized gods, and that the names of the runes were early forms of the names of these gods. This is my own belief. Unfortunately, since so much of the early Teutonic religion has been lost—forgotten before anyone possessed the skills to write it down—this suspicion cannot be proved. Whether or not all the runes were recognized formal gods, though, they behave in magic as divine powers of nature, exhibiting a vitality and independence of action that set them apart from all other magical symbols.

Each rune is the occult name and sigil of one of the most fundamental forces of existence. They touch the very roots of the world tree, *Yggdrasill*, that lie far beneath the topsoil of human perceptions. By working the runes the magus is able to shake the utmost foundations of the universe. This gives runes a power of transformation that is awesome to contemplate. Had it not been for the suppression of rune magic by the Church, it would undoubtedly be the dominant form of magic practiced in the modern West.

The destruction of the living heritage of rune lore by early Christian bishops set rune magic back and delayed its preeminence among occultists. The magics of Egypt and Greece took center stage in the Middle Ages because written records describing their methods had been preserved by respected classical authors such as Virgil and Apuleius. It is only in the present century that the fragments of rune lore, preserved on relics, monuments and in ancient manuscripts, have been collected together and made widely available in the English language. This has made it possible for working occultists well-versed in universal principles of magic to reconstruct the methods of ancient rune magic, and to reinterpret the true meanings of the rune symbols. Rediscovery of runes goes on around the world as you read these words. It is the single most important work in occultism in this century.

WHAT MAKES RUNES SPECIAL?

Wind thou these,
Weave thou these,
Cast thou these all about thee.
— *Volsunga*

Runes are the manifest symbols through which rune magic is worked. They can be employed for all of the purposes that other magical systems serve, but possess unique aspects that make them superior for certain uses.

Because they were forged over the centuries in the same creative fire that shaped the pagan gods of the Teutonic peoples, runes are indispensable in magical dealings that involve the northern hierarchy. They are a key that unlocks the powers of these gods, and a book that unfolds the secrets of their personalities. Before the rediscovery of runes, the *Aesir*, lords of Asgard, who number among their ranks *Odin*, *Thor*, *Tiw*, *Heimdall*, *Baldar*, *Loki*, *Frija* and *Hel*, were difficult to integrate into modern ceremonial magic. An elemental wildness distinguishes them from the more civilized gods of Greece and Rome and the abstract, almost technical natures of the angels and spirits of Hebrew occultism. It would be absurd to invoke the Aesir with Hebrew numerology or Greek barbarous words. Yet before the rebirth of runes, the magus had little option.

Runes form the magical language of the northern gods and express the forces upon which those gods are framed; manipulating them gives direct control over the actions not only of the deities, but also of the spirits and lesser entities of Norse mythology, all of whom arose from the same primeval crucible of mythic archetypes. The runes are more than just arbitrary symbols chosen to represent occult forces by Germanic shamans; each rune contains in its structure the same essence that is in the god, spirit, or magical potential to which it corresponds. It is the magical *name* of that god or natural power.

Anyone seeking to contact and communicate with the northern hierarchy—whether for purposes of worship, divination or active magic—must use the runes. It is possible to invoke the Aesir without runes, but this is akin to driving a nail with a rock when a hammer is sitting within easy reach. It makes no sense. More and more, those with Teutonic roots are seeking to know the gods of their ancestors. Runes are indispensable in building this bridge to the past.

Perhaps because they rested forgotten for so many centuries, the runes remain undiluted by modem skepticism and rationalization. Of all the symbolic tools of magic, they are the most powerful for causing material change in the world. Rune magic makes things happen—often violently, sometimes unpredictably. Most potent physically, rune magic is also most dangerous to the unwary. The elemental powers contained and defined by the runes are not conscious in the human sense, but possess a type of animation and awareness not unlike the self-awareness of animals, plants or embodied spirits—a watchful, quick, sometimes malicious awareness that might almost be called "mad" in its unexpectedness—but madness is a human concept, and the runes are true to themselves and terribly sane.

All types of occult work that seek material change, or transformations on the human level of emotions and urges linked to the body, can be fulfilled with rune magic. Rune magic also embraces the spiritual level of the human soul; great works of the spirit are also possible using the runes. The point here is that runes are weighted more toward the physical, tangible end of the scale than any other ancient magical system. It may be that in their beginnings all magical systems were mainly concerned with material change, but only the runes have descended through time in their pristine, primitive state.

Another unique aspect of the runes is their structure. Because they are simple letters that can be carried in the head and inscribed on any surface, they are the most compact and accessible of magical systems. Bulky temple instruments are not needed in rune magic. Runes can be written anywhere on virtually anything in moments when an emergency arises. No one can ever take the runes away or destroy them; they live in the mind.

In their portability runes resemble the Hebrew letters, which are combined into magical names and words of power based upon the letters' numerical values in the system of Jewish occultism known as the *Kabbalah*. At one time each letter of the Hebrew alphabet also had an elemental meaning independent of its numerical value, but in modern centuries the natural powers embodied in the Hebrew letters have largely been forgotten, displaced by their number values.

As is true of the Hebrew letters, the runes can be combined both in numerical and symbolic occult groupings and phonetically to form words and sentences. The same runes can embody a magical desire in their combination of elemental potentials and explicitly define that desire in words. These methods complement and support each other, and are frequently encountered together on rune artifacts made for magical purposes. For example, the sixth-century Lindholm amulet of Sweden bears the intelligible inscription of its magician-maker: "I am an Herulian, I am called the Cunning One"; it also bears a string of runes that cannot be translated, because they convey an occult, not a literal meaning (see *Rune Magic*, p. 24, where the Lindholm amulet is pictured and described).

WHERE DID RUNES COME FROM?

> *The first charm I know*
> *Is unknown to all*
> *Of any human kind.*
>
> —*Havamal*

Over the last century or so, several theories have arisen on the origin of the runes, each having drawn a strong body of supporters at different times. The nineteenth-century Danish rune scholar L. F. A. Wimmer, struck by the obvious similarity between certain runes and Latin letters, put forward the notion that a single German scribe, using the Latin alphabet as a guide, created the runic alphabet around the time of Christ for the purpose of written communication.

This has historic parallels—Wulfila created the Gothic alphabet for the West Goths in the fourth century. The idea that the runes were invented by one man was quite popular among academics because it eliminated so many difficult questions as to how and why they had come into being.

Another popular theory, put forward by the Scandinavian scholar Friesen around 1900, is that Gothic merchants created the runes in the third century on the shores of the Black Sea for the purpose of trade, taking as their model the Greek alphabet with some admixture of the Latin. This gained many supporters in English-speaking nations because it was included in the influential *Encyclopaedia Britannica* (1929 edition).

In the 1930s, when the nationalist fervor of Nazi Germany reached its fanatical peak, German scholars attempted to prove that runes were purely Aryan in origin, and that they owed nothing to the alphabets of Greece and Rome. Additionally, they claimed that all alphabets around the world were born from the Stone Age prototypes of the runes. These theories were inspired by the mystical writings of Guido von List and Friedrich Bernhard Marby in the nineteenth century. After the Second World War, these ideas were generally ridiculed.

The theory now put forward most often to explain the birth of runes is that a tribe of German mercenaries crossed the Alps into northern Italy in the fourth century B.C., where they practiced their martial trade for some generations. They would have carried a knowledge of the primitive magical symbols used by their shamans with them. In their new land a fusion took place between the magic symbols and their meanings and the letters of the Etruscan alphabet, then in use in northern Italy. Around the second century B.C., knowledge of runes passed back over the Alps and was disseminated through Germany by the Cimbri tribe. At some time in their early development, perhaps around the time they began to be used for writing, the runes must have been strongly influenced by the Latin alphabet, as the similarity between some runes and Latin letters is too obvious to be denied.

A few academics go so far as to deny that runes ever had a significant occult function, but it is generally agreed that in the early centuries of their use they were primarily magical tools, and remained strongly linked to magic throughout their history. Only in their decadence did their use as a script for recording information become widespread. Even then, runes were never the main instrument of written communication. They were inscribed on stone monuments, weapons and other artifacts—and placed in burial mounds—precisely because they *were* magical. The runes magical associations lent authority to any message written with them. It was the voice of the gods speaking to the reader, in a script as holy as Latin (until recent years the sacred language of the Catholic Church).

Once their usefulness as instruments of magic became known to the Teutonic tribes, runes spread like wildfire across northern Europe. One tribe called the Heruli specialized in rune magic, so much so that long after the tribe ceased to exist "Herulian" was a byword for "rune master." The runes were carried by the Saxons to England; from there they quickly spread into Scandinavia and Iceland.

The Vikings took the runes on their world-spanning voyages and left them as graffiti in many unexpected corners of the ancient world. Runes have been discovered in such diverse places as Piraeus in Greece, Berezanji on the Black Sea, Ireland, Scotland, the Hebrides, the Isle of Man and Baffin Bay in Greenland. There has even been speculation that the Vikings left runes in Nova Scotia and Minnesota, but no credible evidence has been found to support either of these claims.

Runes survived longer in Scandinavia (and longest of all in Iceland) not because these lands were especially fond of them but because they resisted more strongly attempts by the Church to suppress pagan religions and customs. This is the only reason that runes, and the northern gods themselves for that matter, are identified with Scandinavia. Runes are a German invention. They reached their greatest refinement as a magical system with the German *futhark* (a word coined from the first six German runes) in the eighth century, after which they began to be adapted to suit regional language requirements and lost some of the clarity of their structure.

The "death" of the runes as magical instruments occurred in 1639, when they were banned by the official laws of Iceland. Those found with runes in their possession were burned alive. By this date they had long since ceased to be anything but a curiosity to the rest of the world, where reference to them would have elicited the same blank stare that it does from the average person today. It is fortunate that a few passing references were made about rune use in the Icelandic sagas, and in some Old English poems. Otherwise, we would know nothing about runes and would not have enough information to understand them.

HOW MANY KINDS OF RUNES ARE THERE?

> *These be the book-runes*
> *And the runes of good help,*
> *And all the taboo-runes*
> *And the runes of much might.*
> *—Volsunga*

Runes had their birth among the barbarian German tribes in northern Italy, perhaps as early as 500 B.C. Around 300 B.C. they somehow found their way over the Alps into Germany, where they continued to develop. The final form of the German rune alphabet was fixed no later than 200 A.D. During the period from roughly 300 to 500 A.D. the Heruli and other tribes specializing in magic carried the runes far and wide. Before there was such a thing as the Scandinavian rune alphabets, the German rune alphabet was being used in Scandinavia. By the eighth century, changes in languages and the wide geographical separation of the runes made local evolutions inevitable.

The process had already begun among the Saxons, who carried a modified twenty-eight character rune alphabet adapted to their language needs with them as they migrated into England. During the ninth century the number was increased to thirty-three runes, but this late addition was confined to Northumbria. In the far north the Danes, Swedes and Norwegians reduced their runes to sixteen, choosing to double up several or more sounds in single runes. Two rune alphabets emerged that are very similar, the Danish and the Swedish-Norwegian.

For magical purposes, the Scandinavian rune alphabets are undesirable because so many of the original runes have been lost, and the ones that remain have suffered radical simplifications in their shapes. The Old English rune alphabets do not suffer from these defects, and have even acquired a measure of respectability in their centuries of use, but there are valid deterrents to using them. The runes added by the Saxons to the end of the German futhark have uncertain occult roots, and there is a possibility that these new runes may distort the magical structure of the German futhark (most clearly evident in its division of the twenty-four runes into three *aettir*, or families, of eight runes each).[1] One of the Northumbrian runes, *Cweord* , (ᛢ) does not even possess a recognized meaning, and no scholarly source that I have consulted is so bold as to suggest one.

The English, and those of English descent, may wish to use the Old English *futhorc* (so called because of differences in pronunciation of the first six runes) of twenty-eight characters, particularly if they are involved in the Wicca tradition. The futhorc has the advantage of being more closely connected with the English language, making the transliteration of English words into runes easier. If the thirty-three rune futhorc is to be used, one might try eliminating the *Cweord* rune altogether and make of the eight remaining new runes a fourth *aett*, or family, named "Ac" after the first of the new runes. As far as I know, I am the first to suggest this possibility, which makes very good sense magically.

I see no reason why the Old English names for the runes should not be employed by English-speaking peoples, even when the runes of the German futhark are being referred to, since the first twenty-four runes of the Old English rune alphabet are identical to the runes of the German rune alphabet, with only a few minor variations in form.

---

1. It may be that they descended by a circuitous route from the pre-runic magical symbols created by the Germanic shamans; this is doubtful, however, and impossible to establish.

The following table illustrates the German futhark with the German names and sounds, the Old English futhorc with its names and sounds, and the meanings of the runes:

	German	Names	Sounds	Old English	Names	Sounds	Meanings
	ᚠ	Fehu	f	ᚠ	Feoh	f	Cattle
	ᚢ	Uruz	u	ᚢ	Ur	u	Aurochs
	ᚦ	Thurisaz	th	ᚦ	Thorn	th	Devil
ᚠ	ᚨ	Ansuz	a	ᚩ	Os	o	God
	ᚱ	Raido	r	ᚱ	Rad	r	Riding
	ᚲ	Kano	k	ᚳ	Cen	c	Torch
	ᚷ	Gebo	g	ᚷ	Gyfu	g	Gift
	ᚹ	Wunjo	w	ᚹ	Wyn	w	Glory
	ᚺ	Hagalaz	h	ᚻ	Haegl	h	Hail
	ᚾ	Nauthiz	n	ᚾ	Nyd	n	Need
	ᛁ	Isa	i	ᛁ	Is	i	Ice
ᚾ	ᛃ	Jera	j	ᛡ	Ger	j	Harvest
	ᛇ	Eihwaz	ei	ᛇ	Eoh	eo	Yew
	ᛈ	Perth	p	ᛈ	Peord	p	Apple
	ᛉ	Algiz	z	ᛉ	Eolh	x	Defense
	ᛊ	Sowelu	s	ᚻ	Sigel	s	Sun
	ᛏ	Teiwaz	t	ᛏ	Tyr	t	Courage
	ᛒ	Berkana	b	ᛒ	Beorc	b	Birch
	ᛖ	Ehwaz	e	ᛖ	Eh	e	Horse
ᛏ	ᛗ	Mannaz	m	ᛗ	Man	m	Man
	ᛚ	Laguz	l	ᛚ	Lagu	l	Water
	ᛜ	Inguz	ng	ᛝ	Ing	ng	Fertility
	ᛟ	Othila	o	ᛟ	Ethel	oe	Homeland
	ᛞ	Dagaz	d	ᛞ	Daeg	d	Day
				ᚪ	Ac	a	Oak
		first addition:		ᚫ	Aesh	ae	Ash
				ᚣ	Yr	y	Saddle
				ᛠ	Ear	ea	Earth
				ᛡ	Ior	io	Eel
				ᛣ	Calc	k	Cup
		second addition:		ᚸ	Gar	g	Spear
				ᛢ	Cweord	q	?
				ᛥ	Stan	st	Stone

Although I have shown *Ethel* before *Daeg* in the German futhark for the sake of comparison with the Old English equivalents, it is generally thought that *Ethel* should follow *Daeg* as the final rune of the futhark in its oldest and more correct sequence. (*Daeg* follows *Ethel* in the Old English futhorc.)

The German futhark has two structural features that are very important in magic. These are the rune families and the rune pairs. From earliest times the runes were divided into three aettir of eight runes. The name of each aett is derived from the rune that begins it:

Feoh aett:	ᚠᚢᚦᚨᚱᚲᚷᚹ	Physical level
Haegl aett:	ᚺᚾᛁᛃᛇᛈᛉᛊ	Emotional level
Tyr aett:	ᛏᛒᛖᛗᛚᛜᛞᛟ	Mental level

These aettir are echoed in runic inscriptions. The Grumpan and Vadstena *bractaetes* of Sweden, dated to the sixth century, show the families of runes divided from each other by dots. The Lindholm amulet has *Feoh* repeated eight times in succession, then *Eolh*, *Nyd* and *Tyr* each repeated three times, in a line that contains a total of twenty-four runes. These numbers must have possessed occult significance. The families were considered so important that even after the number of runes was reduced to sixteen in Scandinavia the aettir were retained, containing six, five and five runes respectively.

It is reasonable to speculate that the aettir reflect at least some of the mystical trines of relationships exemplified by the holy trinities of most religions. The naming rune is the father, or patriarch, of each family, and thus rules it. *Feoh* signifies the physical, *Haegl* the emotional, and *Tyr* the mental level of man.

Within the aettir is a second structural feature that reveals itself only when the meanings of the runes are examined. The futhark is made up of twelve consecutive pairs of runes that possess contrasting or complementary meanings. For example, *Feoh* means cattle, a domestic beast, while *Ur* stands for aurochs, a wild beast like a shaggy bull. Hunting the aurochs was a test of courage and strength, and may have been a rite of passage into manhood; cattle, and the human type of cattle, slaves, served as possessions and units of wealth. Thus the *Feoh* rune meant slavery and servility, while the *Ur* rune meant freedom and valor.

For convenience, the rune pairs are tabulated below:

cattle, possession, slavery	ᚠ	ᚢ	aurochs, freedom, virility
a giant, brutality, evil	ᚦ	ᚨ	a god (Odin), wisdom, good
riding, journey, quest	ᚱ	ᚲ	torch, beacon, spirit
gift, offering, sacrifice	ᚷ	ᚹ	glory, joy, attainment
hail, storm, destruction	ᚺ	ᚾ	need, suffering, endurance
ice, winter, changelessness	ᛁ	ᛃ	harvest, autumn, change
yew, strength, service	ᛇ	ᛈ	apple, pleasure, luxury
defense, protection, warding off	ᛉ	ᛊ	solar ray, lightning, punishment
the god Tiw, war skill, courage	ᛏ	ᛒ	birch, sex, love
horse, vehicle, the means	ᛖ	ᛗ	man, rider, the method
water, dreams, illusions	ᛚ	ᛜ	the god Ing, the Earth, growth
day, light, circle	ᛞ	ᛟ	homeland, inheritance, lifetime

CAN RUNES BE USED FOR DIVINATION?

> *When I see aloft a tree*
> *A corpse swinging from a rope,*
> *Then I cut and paint runes,*
> *So the man walks,*
> *And speaks with me.*
>
> *—Havamal*

The earliest allusions to runes concern divination. The Roman historian Tacitus, writing in 98 A.D., describes how the German priests would cut a bough from a tree and divide it into pieces, then distinguish the pieces by carving into their bark "certain marks." The twigs were cast over a white cloth at random, and after the priest invoked the gods, with eyes raised to heaven he would select three of the twigs and read their meanings. It is very likely these divinatory marks were runes.

In modern occultism rune divination has become most closely associated with rune stones, which are not stones at all but small squares of ceramic impressed with runes. There is nothing wrong with putting runes on ceramic, which has an earthy, natural feel, but there is also no ancient precedent for it. Many people are under the mistaken notion that this is the original medium of runes. In pagan times runes were carved into wood for divination, specifically segments of a fresh bough lopped off a fruit-bearing tree such as the apple. In *Rune Magic* I have reconstructed this ancient technique of rune divination as it may have been formally practiced by the pagan priests.

For less formal occasions, should an individual wish to divine for family or friends, or a professional have the desire to use the runes in paid readings, I have invented two new media that are very convenient and easy to use: rune cards and rune dice.[2]

---

2. These are most effective when they are handmade by the person who will use them. The proper way to make the cards and dice is described in *Rune Magic*. For those who do not wish to make them. I have designed rune cards and rune dice, which may be purchased through Llewellyn Publications.

The *Rune Magic Cards* are similar in some ways to the Tarot. Each card shows a rune and two illustrations that convey its active meaning and its symbolic emblem, as well as its number, name, and place in its rune family, or aett. Since the publication of *Rune Magic*, other rune cards have come onto the market. However, they tend to minimize the runes in favor of the images chosen to represent them.

This is a major error. Divinations are done through the runes themselves, which have many possible interpretations—not just the one image selected by the artist who illustrated the cards. In this respect rune cards are unlike the Tarot, which consists mainly of its images. It is a vital distinction apt to be overlooked by those who rely on a colorful representation of the runes.

There is no ancient precedent for putting runes onto cards, because cards did not exist in Europe at the time the runes were being used for magic. However, early playing cards were invented in China at this time, and were very long and slender, shaped more like wands than modern cards. There is also a type of Korean "card" which consists of thin, flat sticks with Korean characters painted on them (see *A History of Playing Cards*, C. P. Hargrave, pp. 6-12). It is possible that all playing cards have their origin in divination sticks similar to rune wands.

The *Rune Magic Dice* are four cubes, each bearing three pairs of runes. The pairs are oriented to the three dimensions of space, and they create interlock-

ing rings of occult energy about the dice through
their revolutions when the dice are cast. Each cube
stands for one of the four occult elements: Fire,
Water, Air and Earth. By casting the dice and reading the four runes that fall uppermost, as well as the
pattern of the dice and the relationships between the
elements, very detailed, lucid readings into general
and specific questions are possible.

It may seem at first that putting the runes on
dice trivializes them, but this is not so. Dice have
been used from time immemorial for divination.
They were employed for this purpose by the
Greeks and Romans, and significantly, by the
ancient Germans, who were avid gamblers as well
as diviners. Roman historians report that the Germans divined by means of "lots." Such lots for the
Romans meant small blocks of inscribed wood, as
were used for divination in their own temple of the
goddess Fortuna. It cannot be proven, but it is at
least possible that something very similar to the
rune dice existed in ancient times.

Runes are unsurpassed for divination because they
represent a set of manifest qualities that are archety-
pal in significance. They define the essential building
blocks of the human conception of the world. They
convey meaning on all levels, and can be interpreted
literally, as trees, cattle, water and so on; personally,
as human virtues and experiences such as dreams,
desires, courage, eloquence and service; or spiritually,
as good, evil, truth, justice, honor and wisdom. On all

levels the message of the runes is explicit, because the
rune symbols arise out of the world of nature. They
possess the clarity and definition of the stones in a
field and the trees on a hilltop. This makes them easier to interpret than the I Ching, the Tarot, or the symbols of geomancy. I have used all major types of
divination, and find that runes speak in a more
straightforward manner than any of them.

CAN RUNES BE USED FOR RITUAL?

> *If the runes are cut to harm me,*
> *The spell is turned,*
> *The hunger harmed,*
> *Not I.*

—*Havamal*

Ritual magic is, and always has been, the primary
use for runes. Divination is only one branch of
magic. Use of the runes for writing was always a
secondary function among the ancient rune masters, more a way of labeling their magical amulets
and talismans than of releasing magical power (the
undecipherable rune series effected such a release).
After the decline of magic and the rise of the
Church, runic writing gained prominence by
default, because it was the only use of runes still
allowed and still remembered. Medieval monks
kept runic writing alive in their manuscripts as a
scholarly hobby.

Enough hints—and they are no more than this—have survived regarding the methods of rune magic that it is possible to reconstruct some of the techniques. Examples of magical objects that have been unearthed by archaeologists, along with a general knowledge of universal magical practices throughout history and around the world, serve as guides. It is important for occult writers to make clear distinctions between their informed speculations about ancient rune magic, their own innovations, and their attempts to synthesize runes into the framework of modern occultism. Too often this is not done.

The synthesis of runes with the universal Western system of ceremonial magic[3] that has come down from the research of the nineteenth-century Order of the Golden Dawn in England is both necessary and inevitable. Research by occultists is going on everywhere as to how the runes can be best integrated into Golden Dawn magic. There is no supreme court of occultism; this is an organic process spread across cultures and will occupy many years. Insights and practices found to be useful will be retained; others will be forgotten.

Attempts have also been made to establish autonomous systems of rune magic that can stand alone. Some of these that have their roots in nineteenth-century Germany are described in *Rune*

---

3. Disseminated most widely by its chief proponent, Aleister Crowley, and incorporated in part into modern Wicca by Gerald Gardner.

Might, by Edred Thorsson, head of the Rune-Gild, an occult organization devoted to magical use of the German futhark.[4]

The singlemost important fragment of rune lore, from a magical point of view, is embodied in a few lines of the epic poem *Havamal.* The god Odin, the mythic discoverer of the runes, says at the beginning of a list of eighteen rune charms (which he enumerates to boast of the depth of his occult knowledge):

> *Know how to cut them,*
> *Know how to read them,*
> *Know how to stain them,*
> *Know how to evoke them,*
> *Know how to send them.*

In these five short lines is the structure of ancient rune magic. They are the steps in a formal ritual process for calling up the powers of the runes and directing those powers to accomplish desired ritual ends.

The first step, cutting, is the physical making of the runes. The second step, reading, creates the runes on the astral level, where the forces of magic most clearly manifest their workings. The third step, staining, involves the ritual shedding of blood

---

4. This is also a fruitful field of inquiry, and will be of most interest to those who find themselves particularly drawn to the runes, either through temperament or racial heritage. In ancient times the runes were independent, complete unto themselves, and they can still function independent of other traditions in the modern world.

to feed the runes and awaken their power. The fourth step, evoking, is the calling of this power forth into the world. The final step, sending, is the directing of the power of the runes to accomplish a specific magical purpose.

All five stages involve ritual acts, which I have reconstructed and set forth in *Rune Magic*. The result is a magical technique of immense power, provided it is conducted with the necessary dedication. Runes are dangerous toys to play with. Of all types of magic, runes present the most hazard, with the possible exception of spirit evocation.

The rune master Egil Skalla-Grimsson makes this point in the eddic *Egil's Saga*, saying:

> *Runes shall a man not score,*
> *Save he can well to read them.*
> *That many a man betideth,*
> *On a mirk stave to stumble.*

The meaning is, if you do not know what you are doing, it is best to leave well enough alone. But Egil intended this warning for dabblers, not for those willing to undertake a serious study of the runes and their proper uses.

To give some idea of how it is possible to understand the ancient rune magic based upon the hints provided by poets and other ancient writers, I will briefly examine a rune charm featured in the *Volsunga Saga*:

> *Learn the bough-runes wisdom*
> *If leech thou lovest;*
> *And wilt wot about wound's searching*
> *On the bark be they scored;*
> *On the buds of trees*
> *Whose boughs look eastward ever.*

Leech lore is medicine. Bough-runes are runes cut on trees. The charm is a treatment for a wound, presumably to prevent death from infection, a fate that must have been all-too-common in the days before penicillin. The runes are to be cut into the tree's bark, as opposed to its roots. "On the buds" means that the runes are to be carved on the new growth of the tree, where the bark is thin and the sap green and flowing. These new shoots are most full of the tree's vital life-force. "Whose boughs look eastward ever" signifies that the cutting is to be made from a tree growing upon the eastern slope of a hill. It should be a tree exposed to morning sunlight, and the cutting should be made at sunrise.

Once the rune wand had been prepared, it would be carried to the sick person and placed into, or under, his or her bed. The vitality of the tree—a large, strong one would naturally be chosen—fed the runes and empowered them for their curative purpose (defined by the runes themselves and the ritual conducted by the rune master).

Such matters are more than merely academic because of the immense potential of the runes.

Uncontaminated by the scientific world, with its justifications, rationalizations and scientific explanations, that tend to level even the most exalted mystical truths, runes plunge deep beneath the surface of the unconscious sea. Runes liberate a river of spiritual power. They strike at the root of being, far beneath the thin veneer of ego-awareness that modern man mistakenly believes to be the self. The forces set in motion by runes are primal. This is what makes them dangerous. It also makes the runes effective.

WHY DO RUNES HAVE A BAD REPUTATION?

> *Better not to ask than to overpledge*
> *As a gift demands a gift,*
> *Better not to slay than to slay too many.*
> *—Havamal*

Runes have always been mysterious and forbidding. The very word *rune* means a secret or mystery. In popular folklore runes are dangerous, evil, pitiless and destructive. The excellent supernatural story *Casting the Runes* by M. R. James plays up all these legendary aspects. How did the runes get so wicked a reputation?

Part of it can be attributed to their magical efficacy. Rune magicians were feared for their power to command and destroy. Each time the might of the runes was revealed through an act of magic, their authority grew. Coupled with this is the natural human tendency to fear what is not understood. The mystery of the runes heightened their dreadfulness. In the Middle Ages everybody believed in magic, and runes, the most secret and most potent system of magic, was the most feared.

Once the Church had solidified its power in the north to the point that it felt confident in attacking the pagan gods and branding them as devils, it is not surprising that runes came under especially severe censorship. As previously mentioned, just carrying the runes was enough to get you burned alive in Iceland as late as the seventeenth century. This kind of absolute suppression is impossible to emerge from unscathed. It is amazing that runes survived as long as they did, and a tribute to their potency. As more and more common people renounced the old gods and embraced Christ, few were dedicated or brave enough to seek out and preserve the vanishing wisdom which had been handed down from master to disciple, communicated from mouth to ear in solitude.

Runes became associated with stories of human sacrifice that probably had their foundation in kernels of truth. The Druids did sacrifice men in Gaul, as Julius Caesar attests in his *Gallic Wars*. Although the Druids were a Celtic order, it is certain they would have known rune magic. Druids were the most learned pagan scholars of their day. Their order was based in England but extended into Gaul, and they were notorious as magicians among the Romans. Recent archaeological evidence suggests that the Vikings also sacrificed men ritually, although not on a wide scale. Tacitus in his *Germania* speaks of the German slaves who purified the ritual chariot of the goddess Hertha on her sacred island, after which they were drowned as sacrifices.

The Church and her newly converted did nothing to minimize this connection between rune magic and human sacrifice, as can be seen from this passage from the Old English poem *Andreas:*

> *Casting lots they let them decree*
> *Which should die first as food for the others.*
> *With hellish acts and heathen rites*
> *They cast the lots and counted them out.*

This sort of extreme hysteria was the rule rather than the exception once the popes gained confidence in their power, and it goes far to explain the utter annihilation of runes as a magical system. Runes were anathema both to the priests from Rome and to their zealous converts. It is always the way that those inspired by religious fanaticism repudiate most strenuously the very practices which they themselves formerly believed in and followed. There is no stauncher prohibitionist than a reformed alcoholic.

With the rise of the Romantic movement in eighteenth-century Germany (it started somewhat earlier on the Continent than in England), those most romantic of cultural relics, the runes, were rediscovered. Unfortunately there was very little accurate information readily available, and several crackpot schemes and notions gained currency.[5]

Even so, runes remained an integral part of German occultism through the nineteenth and early twentieth centuries, while being virtually ignored in English-speaking nations.

The adoption of runes by those preaching doctrines of Aryan purity and the supremacy of the master race—doctrines embraced with enthusiasm by the Nazi movement—dealt another blow to the reputation of the runes, one that endures to the present day. In fact the Nazis were not very good occultists, but their use of some runes and related symbols tainted them in the world mind.

For example, when I designed the *Rune Magic Cards,* I put a swastika on the card for the rune *Sigel* (⚡), the Sun. The swastika is an ancient symbol of solar force found all over the world. In Teutonic myth it stands for the flaming meteor of Thor's hammer, which is supposed to have fallen from the Sun. Thor is a solar deity. I indicated a swastika turning in a positive sunwise direction, the opposite of the Nazi emblem. Even though the swastika is the most appropriate symbol to represent the active power of the *Sigel* rune (which of course was the sign of the

---

5. Some of these are described by Edred Thorsson in *Rune Might.*

dreaded SS), I knew when I put it on the card that it would be misinterpreted by many of those who saw it as an evil or even racist symbol. I was forced to make a choice as to whether I would allow my action to be dictated by the ignorance of the general population or by the appropriateness of the symbol. It was a difficult choice. This is the continuing legacy of the centuries of unreasoning fear and detestation that still cling to the runes.

Eventually the runes will purge themselves of their evil connotations, at least among occultists, as they become so common that they are understood for themselves and not for the destructive baggage of the vicious rumors and corrupting fables presently encumbering them. But this process may take decades. Every user of the runes must person-ally come to terms with their legend in his or her own mind.

WHAT IS RUNE MEDITATION?

Thought runes shalt thou deal with,
If thou wilt be of all men
Fairest-souled wight and wisest.
—*Volsunga Saga*

Before the runes can be effective for works of magic or divination, they must be understood on the intu-itive level and made to come alive in the uncon-scious. This will occur over time simply by using them, but the process can be encouraged through regular meditation upon the individual rune symbols. Meditation gives the runes reality in the astral world, where magical forces and actions manifest themselves most clearly to the awareness.

When you carve a rune materially for a magical purpose, you must also be able to cut it into the astral with your will, so that it glows and shimmers on the material where you made the physical rune. When you draw a rune in the air with your right index finger or magic wand, you must be able to see it sustaining itself with the eye of your imagination. This does not mean that you pretend to yourself that the rune exists on the astral level, or picture it there in the way you would imagine the face of your cat. Magical visualization is more intense and real than regular images in the imagination. The magical image persists and can be so real that it appears material.

Meditation on the runes serves the dual purposes of expanding understanding of their meanings, both conscious and unconscious (important in divination), and of allowing the clear formation of the runes on the astral level (necessary in ritual magic).

There are many ways to actively meditate upon the runes. One is to contemplate the forms of the runes visually. I have described this technique in the instruction booklet that accompanies the *Rune Magic Cards*. Rune cards are an excellent way of keeping images of the runes before the sight during meditation; once the mind reaches a receptive state, the images impress themselves through the eyes upon the mind.

Here I will describe a second technique that I find effective in bringing the meanings and forms of the runes alive. In preparation you must be familiar with the shapes of the runes, their names and short meanings, their order, the place of each rune in its aett, and each rune's pair. This can be done by playing with a set of rune wands, or ideally with the rune cards, which are excellent for this purpose. Once you have a general knowledge of the futhark, you are ready to begin considering the runes individually.

To be most effective, meditations should be done in a series at regular times, one per day. It is possible to do two meditations a day if they are separated in time—for example, one at noon and one at midnight. If this is done, a pair of runes should be considered each day. However, until you have had some experience in meditating upon the individual runes, you should not attempt to consider two or more runes in combination at the same time.

Wear loose clothing and take off your shoes, belt, watch, jewelry and anything else that distracts, irritates the skin or restricts the circulation. When the mind is stilled and focused, small sounds will seem like thunder and the slightest itch will become a torment as your mind, like a restless child, seeks any escape from the task you have imposed upon it.

Do not meditate where there is any noise or bustle, or where you are likely to be disturbed. Do not meditate until after at least two hours past eating a meal. Do not meditate just before sleep when you are very tired, and do not meditate when you are physically ill, or when your mind is filled with worry, anger or frustration.

Find a tranquil place and sit comfortably with your back relaxed but straight. It does not really matter how you sit. I usually sit Japanese-style upon my heels, but some people find this posture hard on the knees. The important thing is that you forget about how you are sitting and concentrate on the meditation. Face a blank wall or featureless surface. If there is no flat unbroken surface, turn out the lights and the darkness will serve. If you are outside, face a wall, a distant forested hill, or the ocean horizon. Failing that, lie on your back and look at the sky (although it is best not to make a habit of lying down during meditation). The important thing is that you not be distracted by something in your field of view. Distractions are not necessarily fatal to meditations, but they disrupt them and delay progress. There are bound to be distractions—you want to minimize them.

Take half a dozen slow, deep breaths to clear your lungs and relax your body. When you are ready, extend your right index finger and draw the rune you have chosen for your meditation in the air at a comfortable arm's length, making it a size that will fit easily into the center of your field of vision—about eighteen inches tall is a good height.

Now try to actually see the rune in the air where you have drawn it. Hold the form of the rune in your imagination, and mentally retrace over and over the rune you have drawn whenever its strokes become indistinct or slip from your mind. It is not necessary to use your finger to retrace the rune. Pretend you have a blackboard in your imagination, and an imaginary piece of chalk that you use to continually redefine the rune as it fades.

Runes should always be drawn, both in the world and in the mind, with strokes that move downward and to the right. A little practice will make this second nature.

During the meditation do not actively try to consider a predetermined list of associations with the runes. These will rise in their own time and order into the stillness of your consciousness. Hold your attention upon the shape of the rune and your task of keeping it visually before your inner sight. You must not be thinking of your grocery list while you are doing this. It is inevitable that your mind will wander to other things, but when it does, gently and firmly guide it back to the purpose of the meditation—active contemplation of the rune you have drawn in the air. When an idea about the rune itself, its nature, or its relationship to other runes comes into your mind, consider it, but do not try to force these ideas. Let them arise by themselves.

This meditation should be stopped before it becomes physically tiring. There is no point in forcing the work. A period of fifteen minutes to half an hour is about right for most people. Take care that you remain relaxed, your breathing is regular, and your eyes are focused normally, without strain. Strain of any kind is counterproductive. Only sustained attention is required; you will find that this is effort enough.

Success is not marked by how many new ideas you have about the rune, nor even by how clearly you are able to visualize its form in space, but rather by how sustained and effortless your awareness of the rune has been during the period set aside for the exercise.

It is a good idea to do these meditations in the same place and at the same time of day. Several meditations, even half a dozen, should be done on each rune, but these can be mixed up with other runes. You do not have to meditate upon the same rune for six days running—unless you want to, of course. It can be useful to consider the runes in groups, by doing them in pairs, or families, or even by doing the complete futhark on twenty-four consecutive days, and then repeating it several times. If the sequence of meditations becomes tedious, mix it up. Boredom should be minimized, because your mind will seize on any excuse to stop these exercises.

You will probably discover that your mind is without discipline—not even that its discipline is low, but that it does not have any discipline at all. If you try to force it too hard, it will turn around and bite you. You will accomplish nothing. Firmness, patience, persistence and an understanding of how your mind functions are needed to achieve the best results. Be wary of the little tricks. You may suddenly find that your stomach is churning every time you sit down to meditate, that your ears itch, that people are constantly interrupting you, that you feel very tired and sleepy, or that the entire exercise seems pointless and stupid. These are all ways your mind will try to squirm out of doing the work you have set for it.

The rune poems at the end of my book *Rune Magic* were received during a series of meditations upon the individual runes that I undertook on twenty-four consecutive nights. You may find that reading the poem for a particular rune just before meditation upon that rune will awaken new insights.

IS RUNE MAGIC DIFFICULT?

For Woden took nine glory twigs,
He smote the adder that it flew into nine parts.
　　　　　—*Nine Herbs Charms*

Magic is an art, and the magician an artist. It is no less difficult for a skillful magician to perform a rune magic ritual than it is for a trained painter to produce a portrait. Anyone can produce some kind of drawing with a pencil and paper, even if they have no artistic skill; so can anyone walk through the mechanical requirements of a ritual. In both cases, whether the end result has any vitality depends entirely on the training and inherent talent of the artist. The good news is, however, that you do not have to be Michelangelo to draw a bowl of fruit, or Merlin to cast a ritual circle.

The key is practice. Only by trying rituals yourself and performing them many times can you begin to judge whether magic is a worthwhile discipline. Some people are natural magicians. They practice magic constantly without the least awareness of what they are doing. Others are constitutionally unsuited to this sacred art. Their views are materialistic, their opinions set in concrete, all their perceptions fixed upon the physical. There are certain inescapable requirements for a magical personality. You must be sensitive to the world around you and able to receive new perceptions. You must have some imagination. When you see a blue cow in the road in front of you, you must be willing to acknowledge to yourself that it is blue.

Modern rune rituals are sometimes done entirely by visualization—the runes are made in the astral world and never actually written down or carved on any material. This technique can work fairly well, but is not in harmony with the ancient practice. In

ancient times one of the constants of rune magic was
that to even be runes, they had to be marked physically upon some surface. Only when the runes were
made manifest could their power manifest itself in
the world. Because this was the belief of the pagan
rune masters, I will describe how to make a material
rune amulet for help and protection. You can carry it
with you wherever you go. This will also illustrate
some practical aspects of rune magic.

First, you must convert your name into a bind-
rune sigil. Bind runes are single runic characters
made up of two or more runes that share common elements. For example, the ancient bind rune
(ᛘ), combines (ᛗ) and (ᚱ). Write down the letters of your name in a row on a piece of paper,
using your true name, the name you use and have
accepted as your own. In most cases this is the
given and family name. Do not use a formal name
if you have accepted a shortened nickname as
your own. When there is some doubt, choose that
version of your name you feel most comfortable
with. Usually this will omit middle names and
initials, but not in all cases. If you are an initiated
occultist you may wish to use your magical name,
but only if it is truly the most personal expression
of your identity.

Look back to the chart of runes given earlier and
find those corresponding to the letters of your
name in the German futhark. Some accommoda-
tions may have to be made. Not all the sounds in

the English alphabet are in the German runes. Use *Kano* (*Cen*) for *c* and *q* as well as *k*; use *Wunjo* (*Wyn*) for *v* and *w*; use *Algiz* (*Eolh*) for *x* and *z*. If your name contains an *ng*, *th* or *ei*, use the single runes for these sounds. Write down the runes over the letters in your name.

As an example, consider the name Tom Jones. This would be written with the runes above it this way:

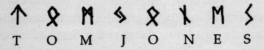

T   O   M   J   O   N   E   S

Now form a single bind rune combining all of the runes in the name. It is not necessary to represent twice those strokes that overlap, but only that you are able to trace completely any rune in the name by following lines in the bind rune. Extending the example, the bind rune for Tom Jones might look like this:

Whatever your bind rune is, it becomes your personal sigil, embodying in symbolic form your individual essence. As you work magic on the bind rune, you are working it on your own ego-self—the part of you that says this is who I am, this is what I want, this is where I am going.

Before working the actual ritual that will create and empower your amulet, practice drawing the bind rune of your name until you have it memorized. Remember, use strokes that run down and to the right. Discard these practice sigils after deliberately destroying them: never leave them lying around.

You will need an open space to work the ritual that will create and empower your amulet. It must be safe from disturbances and intrusions, as well as from discordant associations such as bright colors, posters, scents, background sounds and clutter. Those accustomed to working magic can use their regular ritual temple and its corresponding astral temple. Into the ritual space put a small table as a work surface and altar. (Bedside tables are an ideal size and shape.) If you do not have a table to use, all you really need is a board or other flat surface to write on. Get a new white candle and place it in a short, stable holder so that you can set it upon the table during the ritual.

From a new sheet of paper cut a three-inch square. High quality paper should be chosen—you will want the amulet to last. Single sheets of calligraphy-quality parchment paper can often be bought in stationery stores. Parchment is ideal. Also buy a new pen with red ink; ballpoint is fine.

The pen must be unused, though, and not previously owned by anyone else.

In magical works the runes are always marked in red to symbolize the blood of sacrifice. The ancient rune masters believed that blood fed the runes—or more precisely, the spirit forces manifesting through the runes. It is interesting that many modern voodoo worshippers share an identical belief regarding the spirits in their voodoo drums, which are periodically fed. Blood is not strictly necessary in rune magic and need not be used for most of its rituals. It is not needed in making this amulet.

The ritual should be performed on Wednesday, the day sacred to Odin, father of the northern gods and mythic discoverer of runes. Before beginning, bathe and put on clean, loose clothing. Pajamas or a loose bathrobe will serve. Prepare yourself physically and emotionally as you would if you were about to make love to a person you respected and wished to honor.

Enter the ritual place. Put the pen and paper on the table serving as the altar. Ideally it should be in the center of the space. If there is not enough room to move around it, then put it in the south. Light the candle in the center of the altar top. Stand in the north facing the altar. It is best if the candle is the only light.

Raise your right hand and mentally project a stream of astral fire from your index finger, drawing it from a reservoir in your heart center, and with it form a ring around the ritual space that floats in the air at the level of your heart. Begin the ring of fire at the south and proceed sunwise, taking care to join the end of the ring with its beginning in your visual imagination. Project this magic circle by walking around the altar if you have enough room; if not, pivot on your own axis and mentally extend the ring from your place before the altar. Speak these words, or words like them:

> *I mentally extend this circle of fire*
> *about this place of ritual. Let no evil or*
> *discordant influence enter herein nor*
> *abide within its boundary.*

Stand before the altar with your feet together. With your right index finger draw a large *Os* (ᚠ) rune in the space over the burning candle and visualize it flaming in the air. Spread your arms so that your body forms a great cross. Speak this opening prayer:

> *Mighty Odin, All-Father,*
> *Lord of magic, lord of craft,*
> *Lord of battle, lord of song,*
> *Look with favor upon this charm,*
> *Guide its making, aid its working,*
> *Made in thy blood and in thy name.*

Kneel before the altar. Take up the pen and pass its tip three times lightly through the flame of the candle, taking care that it is not scorched or soiled with soot. Hold the pen with the point down high over the candle in both hands as you continue to visualize the *Os* rune floating in the air above the altar. Speak the words:

> *Blood of valor,*
> *Blood of pain,*
> *Blood of glory,*
> *Mark my name.*

With each of the first three spoken lines, make a sunwise circle with the tip of the pen in the air over and around the candle, moving inward so that the point describes a spiral in three complete revolutions. Visualize at the same time the fire of the *Os* rune streaming down into the back end of the pen and filling it with flaming radiance. The ink in the pen mystically becomes the blood of Odin, which the great god shed in sacrifice during his ordeal to attain the runes. The *Os* rune is completely absorbed into the pen. After you speak the last line, kiss the end of the pen.

With single, firm strokes, draw your personal bind rune sigil in the middle of the square of paper. Visualize the sigil glowing with power. Take up the paper and press it between both your palms in a prayer gesture over your heart as you visualize the sigil you have just inscribed flaming in the center of your chest. Speak the words:

> *By this sign I am known;*
> *My name is _____.*

Speak the name you used in composing the bind rune. Mentally identify yourself with the sigil upon the paper until you feel a unity between yourself and the sigil.

Put the paper back on the altar, and with the pen draw the *Eolh* (ᛉ) rune above the bind rune. Visualize it flickering upon the paper. Speak these words directly to the *Eolh* rune, as you would to a living being:

> *Lord of Eolh,*
> *Grant me protection.*

Draw the *Nyd* (ᚾ) rune below the bind rune, and speak these words to it:

> *Lord of Nyd,*
> *Grant me endurance.*

Draw the *Os* (ᚩ) rune to the left of the bind rune and say to it:

> *Lord of Os,*
> *Grant me eloquence.*

Draw the *Tyr* (ᛏ) rune to the right of the bind rune and say to it:

> *Lord of Tyr,*
> *Grant me courage.*

Pull a single hair out of your head and make the loop of a knot in it without pulling the knot tight. Hold the hair up in both hands and look through the loop at the *Eolh* rune. Slowly pull the loop tight as you say:

> *Power of Eolh,*
> *I bind thee in my service.*

Make a second loop and look through it at the *Nyd* rune so that the ring of hair surrounds the rune. Pull the knot tight as you say:

> *Power of Nyd,*
> *I bind thee in my service.*

Make a third loop, look through it at the *Os* rune and draw it tight, saying:

> *Power of Os,*
> *I bind thee in my service.*

Make a fourth loop, look through it at the *Tyr* rune and draw it tight, saying:

> *Power of Tyr,*
> *I bind thee in my service.*

Visualize the four knots shining with radiant fire like four stars. Place the hair on the bind rune and fold the paper in from the top, and then from the bottom, so that it all overlaps in three layers. Then fold the paper in from the left and from the right. These four creases will result in a one-inch square of nine layers. The hair should be inside touching the bind rune.

Stand up in front of the altar with your feet together and spread your arms so that your body once again forms the sign of a great cross. Speak this closing prayer to Odin:

> *Mighty Odin, All-Father,*
> *Lord of magic, lord of craft,*
> *Lord of battle, lord of song,*
> *I give thanks for the fulfillment*
> *Of this ritual of making.*

In the reverse order that you extended the magic circle, draw it back into your heart center through your left index finger, beginning at the south and turning widdershins—against the course of the Sun—saying as you do:

> *I indraw this flaming circle of power*
> *to my center of being and return this*
> *chamber to its common state.*

Blow out the candle. The folded paper should be put into some case or covering so that it can be carried on the body as an amulet. The ideal holder would be a locket of gold on a long chain that would allow it to be worn about the neck over the heart. Silver will also serve. It is even better if the locket is made specifically to carry the amulet, thereby itself becoming part of the amulet. The paper might also be carried in a wallet or a purse, on a key ring, in a belt or behind a belt buckle, in a shoe or a hat, or in the pocket. Whichever method is chosen, the paper must be protected from wear and perspiration in some kind of sealed holder, or it will soon fall apart. It is best if the case is sealed permanently.

Do not talk about the amulet or show it to others. If you do, it will not work. To avoid the awkwardness of people asking you what it is, carry it out of sight. If someone does ask about the amulet, say nothing. Never let others handle it or touch it. It will function for you and only for you.

At moments when you especially need the power of the amulet, hold it tightly in your left hand. Visualize in the air before you whichever of the four runes best matches your needs. For example, if you are about to have a job interview, write a school examination or a difficult letter, give a public lecture, or try to make an important sale, visualize for a moment the *Os* rune while holding the amulet. This will further magnify and focus its power.

Do not call upon the power of the *Nyd* rune unless you are in a situation of extreme danger or hardship that you cannot escape and must endure to the end. The *Nyd* rune is not gentle or friendly, but may keep you alive when you think you are going to die.

This is a highly effective amulet, but it will work only if correctly made. Right making entails more than merely following the above procedure mechanically. Before even trying to make this charm you must be thoroughly familiar with the meanings of all the runes, and have learned to visualize them clearly through your rune meditations. Practice projecting and indrawing the magic circle. This can be done for prayer or meditation of all kinds. A knowledge of

Odin and his role in discovering the runes is essential. You should read all that is available on rune magic and perform rune divination as a way of getting to know the runes. Ritual work in other fields of magic is, of course, also a great asset.

Most important of all, you must believe completely in what you are doing and conduct the ritual with the greatest possible care and attention to detail. Be serious, and understand in your heart and mind that you are making an important tool that will help you significantly in your daily life.

On the following pages you will find listed, with their current prices, some of the books now available on related subjects. Your book dealer stocks most of these and will stock new titles in the Llewellyn series as they become available. We urge your patronage.

TO GET A FREE CATALOG

To obtain our full catalog, you are invited to write (see address below) for our bi-monthly magazine/catalog, *Llewellyn's New Worlds of Mind and Spirit*. A sample copy is free, and it will continue coming to you at no cost as long as you are an active mail customer. Or you may subscribe for just $10 in the United States and Canada ($20 overseas, first class mail). Many bookstores also have *New Worlds* available to their customers. Ask for it.

TO ORDER BOOKS AND TAPES

If your bookstore does not carry the titles described on the following pages, you may order them directly from Llewellyn by sending the full price in U.S. funds, plus postage and handling (see below).

Credit card orders: VISA, MasterCard and American Express are accepted. Call us toll-free within the United States and Canada at 1-800-THE-MOON.

Postage and Handling: Include $4 postage and handling for orders $15 and under; $5 for orders over $15. There are no postage and handling charges for orders over $100. Postage and handling rates are subject to change. We ship UPS whenever possible within the continental United States; delivery is guaranteed. Always provide your street address, as UPS does not deliver to P.O. boxes. Orders shipped to Alaska, Hawaii, Canada, Mexico and Puerto Rico will be sent via first class mail. Allow 4-5 weeks for delivery. **International orders:** Airmail - add retail price of each book and $5 for each non-book item (audiotapes, etc.); Surface mail - add $1 per item.

Minnesota residents please add 7% sales tax.

Llewellyn Worldwide
P.O. Box 64383-829, St. Paul, MN 55164-0383, U.S.A.
For customer service, call (612) 291-1970.

RUNE MAGIC
by Donald Tyson

Drawing upon historical records, poetic fragments, and the informed study of scholars, *Rune Magic* resurrects the ancient techniques of this tactile form of magic and integrates those methods with modern occultism so that anyone can use the runes in a personal magical system. For the first time, every known and conjectured meaning of all 33 known runes, including the 24 runes known as "futhark," is available in one volume. In addition, *Rune Magic* covers the use of runes in divination, astral traveling, skrying, and on amulets and talismans. A complete rune ritual is also provided, and 24 rune words are outlined. Gods and Goddesses of the runes are discussed, with illustrations from the National Museum of Sweden.

0–87542–826–6, 224 pgs., 6 x 9, photos $10.95

THE NINE DOORS OF MIDGARD
A Complete Curriculum of Rune Magic
by Edred Thorsson

The Nine Doors of Midgard are the gateways to self-transformation through the runes. This is the complete course of study and practice which has successfully been in use inside the Rune-Gild for fifteen years. Now it is being made available to the public for the first time.

The runic tradition represents a whole school of magic with the potential of becoming the equal of the Hermetic or Cabalistic tradition. The runic tradition is the Northern or Teutonic equivalent of the Hermetic tradition of the south. *The Nine Doors of Midgard* is the only manual taking a systematic approach to initiation into runic practices.

Through nine lessons or stages in a graded curriculum, the book takes the rune student from a stage in which no previous knowledge of runes or esoteric work is assumed to a fairly advanced stage of initiation. The book also contains a complete reading list of relevant outside material.

0-87542-781-2, 320 pgs., 5-¼ x 8, illus. **$12.95**

NORTHERN MAGIC
Mysteries of the Norse, Germans & English
by Edred Thorsson
This in-depth primer of the magic of the Northern Way introduces the major concepts and practices of Gothic or Germanic magic. English, German, Dutch, Icelandic, Danish, Norwegian, and Swedish peoples are all directly descended from this ancient Germanic cultural stock. According to author Edred Thorsson, if you are interested in living a holistic life with unity of body-mind-spirit, a key to knowing your spiritual heritage is found in the heritage of your body—in the natural features which you have inherited from your distant ancestors. Most readers of this book already "speak the language" of the Teutonic tradition.

Northern Magic contains material that has never before been discussed in a practical way. This book outlines the ways of Northern magic and the character of the Northern magician. It explores the theories of traditional Northern psychology (or the lore of the soul) in some depth, as well as the religious tradition of the Troth and the whole Germanic theology. The remaining chapters make up a series of "mini-grimoires" on four basic magical techniques in the Northern Way: Younger Futhark rune magic, Icelandic galdor staves, Pennsylvania hex signs, and "seith" (or shamanism). This is an excellent overview of the Teutonic tradition that will interest neophytes as well as long-time travelers along the Northern Way.

0–87542–782–0, 224 pgs., mass market, illus. $4.95

THE POWER OF THE RUNES
A Complete Kit for Divination & Magic
by Donald Tyson

This kit contains *Rune Magic*, Tyson's highly acclaimed guide to effective runework. In this book he clears away misconceptions surrounding this magical alphabet of the northern Europeans, provides information on the gods and goddesses of the runes, and gives the meanings and uses of all thirty-three extant runes. The reader will be involved with practical runic rituals and will find advice on talisman, amulet and sigil use.

This kit also includes the *Rune Magic Deck*. This set of twenty-four large cards illustrates each of the Futhark runes in a stunning two-color format. This is the first deck ever published, which makes it not only unique but truly historical!

In addition, there is a set of four wooden rune dice provided in their own cloth bag. These square dice were designed by Donald Tyson himself. The user casts them down, then interprets their meanings as they appear before him. With the twenty-four Futhark runes graphically etched on their sides, these dice let the user perform an accurate reading in mere seconds.

0-87542-828-2, Boxed set: *Rune Magic*, **24-card deck, 4 dice w/bag** $24.95

A PRACTICAL GUIDE TO THE RUNES
Their Uses in Divination and Magick
by Lisa Peschel

At last the world has a beginner's book on the Nordic runes written in straightforward and clear language. Each of the 25 runes is elucidated through no-nonsense descriptions and clean graphics. Alterations in rune's meaning in relation to other runes, and its reversed position are also included. The construction of runes and accessories covers such factors as the type of wood to be used, the size of the runes, and the coloration, carving and charging of the runes.

With this book, the runes can be used in magick to effect desired results. Talismans carved with runescripts or bindrunes allow you to carry your magick in a tangible form, providing foci for your will. Four rune layouts complete with diagrams are presented with examples of specific questions to ask when consulting the runes. Rather than simple fortunetelling devices, the runes are oracular, empowered with the forces of nature. They present information for you to make choices in your life.

0-87542-593-3, 192 pgs., illus., mass market $3.95

LEAVES OF YGGDRASIL
Runes, Gods, Magic, Feminine Mysteries, and Folklore
by Freya Aswynn

Leaves of Yggdrasil is the first book to offer an extensive presentation of rune concepts, mythology and magical applications inspired by Dutch/Frisian traditional lore.

Author Freya Aswynn, although writing from a historical perspective, offers her own interpretations of this data based on her personal experience with the system. Freya's inborn, native gift of psychism enables her to work as a runic seer and consultant in psychological rune readings, one of which is detailed in a chapter on runic divination.

Leaves of Yggdrasil emphasizes the feminine mysteries and the functions of the Northern priestesses. It unveils a complete and personal system of the rune magic that will fascinate students of mythology, spirituality, psychism and Teutonic history, for this is not only a religious autobiography but also a historical account of the ancient northern European culture.

0-87542-024-9, 288 pgs., 5-¼ x 8, softcover $12.95

RUNE MIGHT
Secret Practices of the German Rune Magicians
by Edred Thorsson

Rune Might reveals, for the first time in the English language, the long-hidden secrets of the German rune magicians who practiced their arts in the beginning of the century. By studying the contents of *Rune Might* and working with its easy-to-use exercises, the reader is introduced to a fascinating world of personalities, as well as the sometimes-sinister, dark corners of runic history. Beyond these findings, the reader is able to experience the direct power of the runes encountered by the early German rune magicians.

Rune Might takes the best and most powerful of the runic techniques developed in the early phase of runic revival and presents them as a coherent set of exercises. Experience rune yoga, rune dance, runic hand gestures (mudras), rune singing (mantras), group rites with runes, runic healing, runic geomancy, and two of the most powerful runic methods of engaging transpersonal powers: the Ritual of the Ninth Night and the Ritual of the Grail Cup.

The exercises represent bold new methods of drawing magical power into your life—regardless of the magical tradition or system with which you normally work. No other system does this in quite the direct and clearly-defined ways that these rune exercises do.

0-87542-778-2, 176 pgs., 5-¼ x 8, illus. **$7.95**

RITUAL MAGIC
What It Is & How To Do It
by Donald Tyson

For thousands of years men and women have practiced it despite the severe repression of sovereigns and priests. Now *Ritual Magic* takes you into the heart of that entrancing, astonishing, and at times mystifying secret garden of *magic*.

What is this ancient power? Where does it come from? How does it work? Is it mere myth and delusion, or can it truly move mountains and make the dead speak...bring rains from a clear sky and calm the seas...turn the outcome of great battles and call the Moon down from heaven? Which parts of the claims made for magic are true in the most literal sense, and which are poetic exaggerations that must be interpreted symbolically? How can magic be used to improve *your* life?

This book answers these and many other questions in a clear and direct manner. It explains what the occult revival is all about, and reveals foundations of practical ritual magic, showing how modern occultism grew from a single root into a number of clearly defined esoteric schools and pagan sects.
0-87542-835-5, 288 pgs., 6 x 9, illus., softcover $12.95